D1744664

WHERE WOULD YOU BE IN 300 EUROS?

LANGUAGE OF FOREX MARKETS

UMUT SASOGLU

CHAPTER ONE

INTRODUCTION

I was close to celebrating my tenth year in Financial Markets, looking back a decade of which I had mostly spent as an FX Trader. It was late 2017 and that is when I had attended a speech of a well-known author, a famous guy who has books about trading and who also teaches people how to trade live on stage. One of my favourite books is written by him and it was the first time I saw him on stage. I must say for a novice in the market, his speech was very informative. For any experienced trader, his speech was a good reminder of things forgotten whilst lost in the noise of daily trading. I would have come out of it elated to a degree if I had not witnessed the following. In the Q&A session, he was asked a question about his own trades and the answer was he wasn't trading at all because he didn't think he was a good trader. A part of me thought "Oh, what a lovely guy, he gave a very honest answer." However, hearing him saying "I don't think I am a good trader" was also a big shock to me! I respect his honesty and I also respect him a lot in many other ways but if the answer was something like "I have traded for many years and I found out that I wasn't a good trader. In my presentations, I am also covering the mistakes I had made throughout the years so that others don't repeat my mistakes", believe me, I would have respected him much more.

"I don't think I am a good trader" made me 'quietly' question whether he had ever traded properly. Had he ever experienced what it felt like to lose or make money on a trade? Had he ever done both several times in one single day and experience the emotional rollercoaster effect? The next question in my mind was whether the guidance on trading and for the purpose of this book, education on FX Markets should be left to people who don't have live experience in the field. The following example might sound extreme but I will use it to make myself clearer. Imagine that you have applied for a driving license, would you really want to learn how to drive from a person who has chosen to isolate himself from big cities, totally against technology but still has memorized a driving license book without having seen how traffic lights actually look like? Or would you rather learn it from a professional driver? I would definitely go for the latter option. He would not only teach me the theory, but he could also talk about real life examples, such as, why some people will drive against the rules and what to do when you see them. Or, why would I hear a car unexpectedly honking for a short time and why would another one once again unexpectedly honk but for a much longer time.

In order to relate the questions above to our topic here, please ask this question to yourself: Is it worth to learn about what actually is going on in currency markets from someone who has professional, emotional and monetary experience in trading billions of dollars throughout the years and who wouldn't waste your time? If your answer is "yes", then please go on reading.

I particularly mentioned "not wasting your time" above, because I kept this book very brief and filled with information which I strongly believe you MUST know. This is one of the reasons why I think this book will be a valuable read for anyone interested in Foreign Exchange Markets and possibly on a broader basis, for anyone who has an interest in Financial Markets. I can't remember how many times I have wasted my time having read a book of hundreds of pages where the main messages could have been written in twenty pages. Although, like anyone else in the planet I like sitting on a sofa and not do anything at all from time to time, but otherwise, I am a big believer in efficient use of time. I can also become obsessed about it depending on what I am spending my time for, but for certain, in this book, I don't want to waste your time talking about similar things over and over again or go too much into detail. Instead, I want to keep everything straight to the point and limit the book with the essentials so that you can read it again or refer back to the relevant topics easily whenever you need to.

Providing you with information which you MUST know is exactly what I am aiming to deliver in this book. I will not only talk about the theory but I will also be aiming to give you insights on how the real world of currency markets look like. It doesn't matter whether you want to trade the markets, or you want to apply for a job in sales, trading, middle office, back office functions, or whether you just think (as I do) that you should somehow know about Forex Markets, I believe you have to know most of the following if not all of them. I encourage you to read till the very end and enjoy!
After finishing this book, first, you should be expanding your knowledge in currency markets and markets overall. Second, you should be able to speak the language of markets. For example, the question "Where would you be in 300 Euros?" will mean different things to a foreign exchange trader, a travel agent, and definitely to a complete stranger in the street. As a person who also somewhat covered the topic of currencies as a part of his Economics education, I strongly believe the next big idea on the subject will come from an academic. However, I am also glad that I have never used terms like "u-s-d-j-p-y" or "dollar over euro" or even "dollar-euro" in my interviews several years ago. I am sure the people working on the theory side of things know many things better than we do, but, I am sorry, that is not the language we use in the markets.

So please take this as a disclaimer, the definitions of the terminology used in this book might not reflect the exact definitions but they are rather how they are used in the markets.

Thirdly, as the saying "sky is the limit" is associated with Forex Markets more often than others, you will also learn different ways of making a life for yourself in the markets and have an idea on whether this is the right business model or the right profession for you.

CHAPTER TWO

BASICS OF FOREIGN EXCHANGE MARKETS

I used the terms Currency Markets, Foreign Exchange Markets, Forex Markets and FX Markets. Is there any difference? The quick answer is NO, they are generally used interchangeably referring to what I will be talking about in this book.

A **currency** as you already know is the medium of exchange officially accepted by governments. (Cryptocurrencies are out of the scope of this book.) Some countries will have their own currencies whereas some others will share a common currency, e.g, the countries in Euro Area (mostly referred as Eurozone or EZ) use "Euro" as their medium of exchange.

G10 vs EM Currencies
If you are involved in currency markets. You will often hear **G10(G11)** and **EM Currencies**. **G10 currencies** refer to 10 currencies which is mostly (not necessarily) used by developed countries.

The full list and 3 letter abbreviations are as below:

1. USD - United States Dollar
2. EUR - Euro
3. GBP - Pound Sterling
4. CHF - Swiss Franc

5. JPY - Japanese Yen
6. AUD - Australian Dollar
7. NZD - New Zealand Dollar
8. CAD - Canadian Dollar
9. NOK - Norwegian Krone
10. SEK - Swedish Krona

If we add DKK which is the Danish Krone to the list, that will make up the G11 currencies.

Among these, AUD, NZD and CAD together are referred as the **Commonwealth currencies** whereas the last three of the list, NOK, SEK and DKK are the **Scandies**. These ones also exemplify why I have put that disclaimer. Obviously, when someone said "Commonwealth" you would not normally think of only 3 countries or 3 currencies, however in world of currency markets if someone is referred as a Commonwealth Trader, first thing that should pop in mind is that he/she trades those 3 currencies as a minimum.

As a generalization, the rest of the currencies would be under **Emerging Markets** or shortly **EM currencies** which are the currencies used mostly if not all by Emerging Market economies. CNH/CNY (China), RUB (Russia), TRY (Turkey), ZAR (South Africa) are some of the important ones in EM space. Group codes for currencies are not limited to G11 currencies. As an example, **CE3** is commonly used as a code name for PLN, HUF, CZK which are the currencies used in Poland, Hungary and Czech Republic respectively. You can also hear the term **CE4** being also very commonly used which is essentially RON of Romania added to CE3 list.

So, now you should already have added these terms in your markets language: EM Salesperson, CE3 Trader or Scandies Research Analyst…

What are other main differences between G10 and EM currencies?

First, the volumes traded in G10 space are generally higher

than EM ones for various reasons. One reason would be the real interest in these currencies. There is no question that a worldwide known big multinational company based in US will sell more products or services to the entire Eurozone than, say, to Hungary alone unless there is a special interest in the country. And thus, you would expect them to convert their euros to dollars in a much larger volume than they do for their forints (HUF) to dollars. Or vice versa, it is normal the expect the total exports of the EZ to US is more than Hungary's exports to US alone. Another reason is the risk element in EM economies which is considered to be usually higher than the developed economies. I will revisit this point later on. These are only two reasons among many others for the differences in traded volumes between G10 and EM currencies.

Here, it will be worth talking about the term **liquidity** as I am sure you will be coming across to this term very often. You can find different definitions of this term but the simple way of describing it is that it is a measure of how easy you can buy or sell a currency pair with minimum market impact. I will revisit the term when we talk about the **bid offer spread** but for now as a general rule of thumb remember that the more volume of buyers and sellers together provide interest to the market, the more liquid a currency pair is.

Now let's focus on the implications of these currencies in Forex Markets. In Forex Markets the currencies are traded in pairs. As an example, you won't see a price for CAD alone but you will see it as USD/CAD. Here the first currency written (in this case USD) is called the **base currency.** The second one (in this case CAD) can be called in different ways such as **counter currency, quote currency, secondary currency** and in some cases (usually for EM currencies) as **local currency**. For every currency, market conventionally trades one particular base more than the others. There are different reasons for that (geographical location, international trade activities, etc.) but for now, at least at a conventional level, remember that USD is one of the largest traded base currency in terms of volume and EUR is the other one for EM currencies. For the G11 list above the conventional way of trading them is as follows:

EUR/USD
GBP/USD, EUR/GBP
EUR/CHF
EUR/JPY
AUD/USD
NZD/USD
USD/CAD
EUR/SEK
EUR/NOK
EUR/DKK

In EM you will see many currency pairs where USD is the base as in USD/TRY but some others will conventionally have EUR base as in EUR/PLN (and the rest of CE4)

Crosses
Does it mean you cannot trade EUR/TRY or CHF/TRY? Of course, you can. Any currency pair including TRY apart from its conventional USD based form will be referred as a **cross.** But the way the big market players trade these is mostly as follows. If I wanted to buy EUR/TRY, I would buy EUR/USD and USD/TRY simultaneously. Why? Because EUR/USD and USD/TRY is generally more liquid than EUR/TRY itself. And once again liquidity is all about easiness of executing these.

If you are confused, let's elaborate this a little bit more with an example. The example might confuse you more but knowing what is actually happening behind the scenes will help you a lot once you understand this. Let's introduce two terms used in the market first.
Long: Buying a currency pair is referred as **going long** in a currency pair.
Short: Selling a currency pair is referred as **going short** in a currency pair.
A quick note: In the world of equities as an example, you don't have to own a share to short sell it, but you are betting for a price decrease in the share. Similarly, in currency markets, if you are going short for a pair, you expect the price to fall

down.

When you buy or go long in EUR/TRY, you are essentially buying EUR and selling TRY. You don't even have TRY to sell right? It is just like that company share you sold without actually owning it. If you are trading the currency markets you can imagine as if you can have a positive and a negative balance in any currency that is available to you. So, say you have an account with an online broker website on which you have deposited USD 400 and you buy 10000 EUR/TRY and EUR/TRY rate is 5, you can think of this as if you bought EUR 10000 and sold TRY 50000. Your theoretical bank account will look like this:

USD +400
EUR +10000
TRY -50000

Please note down those three lines above and let's compare that to how it is done when the volumes are large. In that case the transaction takes place in two phases at the background as mentioned. You will be buying EUR/USD and USD/TRY simultaneously. Let's see how it would look like in this example using similar figures. Let's assume the market rates are EUR/USD 1.25, USD/TRY 4 and EUR/TRY 5. So first you only have USD balance

1) Your initial balance is:
USD +400

You buy 10000 EUR/USD (which is buying EUR 10000 and selling 12500 USD)

2) Your new balance is:
USD -12100   (+400-12500)
EUR +10000

And you buy those USDs back with a USDTRY transaction which is buying USD 12500 and selling 50000 TRY as USD/TRY rate is 4.

<u>3)</u> Your final balance is:
<u>USD +400   (-12100+12500)</u>
<u>EUR +10000</u>
<u>TRY -50000</u>

This is the same result as above, as you can see. Especially, if you are a trader working for a bank, this calculation should help you in a great way.

If you are trading online at home, the broker page will automatically update their systems to show you if you are making or losing money. Let's say EUR/TRY goes to 6 a few hours later (of course this is not a move you would expect in a normal day) and you decide to sell the position back. Now you are selling EUR 10000 back but now you are given TRY 60000. Now your theoretical account will look like this:

<u>USD +400</u>
<u>TRY +10000</u>

If you are trading with an online broker, instead of the above, broker will convert those TRY into USDs and show you your USD balance instead. If the USD/TRY rate is still 4, you have already made USD 2500 in profits so your new account balance will be

USD + 2900

That is the only thing you will be seeing in the system.

CHAPTER THREE

THE LANGUAGE

Going back to the conventions, especially if you are going for an interview you'd better know how the market players 'call' the currencies. I won't be going through each of them but at least knowing that of G10 currencies will be helpful.

Currencies move rapidly in the market and seconds will matter. If you are asking a price in USD/CAD you don't want to be losing time on saying "United States Dollar versus Canadian Dollar". Don't think I am exaggerating here. I am definitely not. You should simply say "dollar kad". Here is the list with roughly how you should be reading them.

USD - Dollar
EUR - Euro as you all know similar to Yuro
GBP - Sterling
CHF - Swiss
JPY - Yen
AUD - Aussie
NZD - Kiwi
CAD - Kad
NOK - Nokkie
SEK - Stokkie/Stocky

It is also for your best interest to know two other things. If someone is only saying Euro but referring to a pair, that would mean EUR/USD. And also, GBP/USD pair is simply read as **cable, but not "sterling dollar"**

Having talked about the speed in markets, if you are in a big institution you won't be hearing anyone using the terms millions or billions. Market language says: "Simply omit millions and instead of billions use **yards.**"

Example: 5,000,000 worth of EUR/USD is read as "five euros" or "five euro dollar" whereas 5,000,000,000 will be "five yards of Euros". You will hear the latter more often in other markets apart from spot FX, e.g., currency swap markets.

We are getting very close to the title of this book. Let's make a bit more ground for that.

Pip: A pip usually refers to the fourth decimal point. Not always but mostly it does. If EUR/USD moves from 1.2500 to 1.2501 we say it moved a pip, likewise if it moves to 1.2510 we say that it is ten pips higher. **A big figure** generally refers to 100 pips. Moving from 1.25 to 1.26 is a big figure move. Also, if anyone asks the big figure for the price in EUR/USD you should say 1.25 or 1.26 or wherever it is. If you buy the pair at 1.2514 you can say "I bought it at 14… 1.25 is the big figure". If you say **"the figure"** alone, it will refer to a level which ends with "00" such as 1.2500. As you can see the last two digits are the ones you should be interested especially if you are a day trader, a treasurer, a broker or a salesperson. People will assume that you know the big figure anyways.

Let's look at the following scenario.

A disclaimer here, this is a made-up scenario and prices do not provide any guidance or any indication to usual market practice. The figures used are totally for market language education purposes.

A treasurer in a multinational corporate company asks the bank on a chat what the price would be in 300,000,000 EUR/USD contacting the salesperson.

Salesperson then calls the trader on a speakerphone.

Treasurer: 300 Eur? (chat) - (I want to see your quotation for 300,000,000 EUR/USD)
Sales: Sure (chat)

Sales: Where are you in 300 Euros? - (What is your price in 300,000,000 EUR/USD)
Trader: Sure, fifteen – twenty-six - (1.2515 - 1.2526)

Sales: 15/26(chat)

Once again please read the disclaimer again especially if you are already a professional in the market and you see wider spreads like 1.2325/1.2725. The spreads will differ depending on various things, liquidity being one of the most important factors if not the most or even the only important one.

Having said **spread,** let's talk about **bids and offers.** A **bid** is the price a trader will be willing to buy a pair for a given volume and an **offer** is where a trader will be willing to sell it. In the above example, trader's bid is 15 and his offer is 26. The difference is called the **bid offer spread** or simply the **spread** which is 11 pips in this case. The **mid** is the middle point between the bid and the offer. As a general rule of thumb, the tighter the spread, the better the liquidity. As you can expect, the spread is usually wider in EM currencies than G10 pairs.

If the treasurer is happy to show his intentions (whether he wanted to buy or sell) he could also have asked "What is your bid in 300 Euros?" or "What is your offer in 300 Euros?". Another way of asking these two questions would be "Where is your **LHS** in 300 Euros?" or "Where is your **RHS** in 300 Euros?" **LHS,** here as you can guess is **"left-hand-side"** which refers to the bid and **RHS** is **"right-hand-side"** which refers to the offer.
If the treasurer's intention was only to check how the bank's perception of liquidity was in a particular time, he could also just ask about that without checking the live price. Asking

"What is your spread in 300 Euros?" or "**How wide** would you be in 300 Euros?" would suffice in this case where the answer would simply be 11. "Where would you be in 300 Euros" is also asking the spread but the client is also after what level the market is at. So, in this situation "15-26" is the good answer, instead of "11"

One quick note: You might think at this point that many things I write seem obvious and needs no explanation. Please remember that it is not only about understanding what these mean. Your purpose should be to know what to say. If I said "what is the gap between your bid and offer…" I know you would understand what it means but it would not be the terminology used in Financial Markets. It is simply "how wide". Nothing else. If you use something different than what I write, people will of course understand what you mean but you will only look like a new grad out of university coming to work wearing a tie to impress people in an office where no one else uses a tie. This would be without noticing that most of the time, the impression he gives will be that he is a junior rather than a high qualified professional. This is not judging a book by its cover but there is a fact that throughout their careers, senior people see hundreds of these juniors wearing ties very often to quit this habit within months if not weeks or even days. So, bottomline is if you want to be in Forex Markets, you'd better learn the language that others in this profession use as soon as possible and look like someone who knows what he/she is talking about.

Now, let's go back to the example above. The trader in the bank is referred as the **market maker**, and the treasurer in the corporate side is the **price taker.** Quoting bids and offers for any given product is called the market making activity. But not all the traders are market makers.

If the treasurer agrees to trade on one of the prices, then the business is called as the **flow** inside the bank. A business between a bank and its client can be in different ways.

1. <u>Market making activities:</u> As mentioned, the client can ask for a bid or offer or both and can deal on the price.
2. <u>Off-market order based activities:</u> Client can give the bank a **Take Profit (T/P) / Limit** or **Stop Loss (S/L)** order. Example: Market is trading around 1.2520. Client might want to buy 300 Euros only if the price reaches 1.2500. Bank will be working to buy at 1.2500. This is a limit order. On the other hand, if the client left an order to buy if the price breaks above 1.2550 that will be called a Stop Loss order. Please note, the name should not mislead you, as in either case, the client doesn't need to have a position before the trade. 1.2550 can also be a **stop-entry,** a price only when reached client thinks there is momentum higher, but for the sake of easiness he just says S/L 300 EUR at 1.2500. A third order will be a **call level** order, where there is no transaction but the client wants to be notified when a price reaches a certain level. This is also referred as "alert" by the online brokerage systems. If you are to become a client to a bank, you might wonder what happens if your level is not triggered and the trader in the bank leaves at the end of the day. FX Markets are open for 24 hours in week days and if you are working with a large enough international bank, your order will either be watched by someone else who is taking the shift, or your order will be transferred over to the next trading hub. Main hubs are London/Europe (that is where most of the business takes place), New York/US and Asia.
3. <u>Orders at the current price level:</u> These are orders where a client calls and tells the bank to buy or sell a currency pair. These used to be called "at best orders" but as the term could be misleading, banks are made to use different terms nowadays.

Let's have a look at the typical conversations which will cover all three cases above. To make it quicker I will cut the treasurer out of the conversation and treat as if it was between the salesperson and the trader of the bank. At the time you read this book I wouldn't be surprised to see all these 3 type of activities to be done by different desks but at least in the early 2000s, all these 3 were done by similar desks and by the same people.

Sales: Where is your offer for 25 EUR/USD?
Trader: Sure. 18 at the moment.
Sales: 1.2518, right?
Trader: Correct… Ref that! Ref that! It is higher!
Sales: OK, where is it now.
Trader: 27…
Sales: Showing…
Trader: Off! Off that. Higher again. Your risk, ask me again!
Sales: No worries you are not at risk, client wants to buy it lower. Where is the market mid at the moment?
Trader: 1.2529 as we speak.
Sales: OK, client wants to work an order. Please work to buy 25 at the figure.
Trader: Sure, working you! To confirm I am working to buy 25 Euros at 1.2500
Sales: Agreed!

2 hours later.

Trader: I bought 5 so far, still working 20 more.
Sales: Sure, let me call the client… Where is the market at the moment?
Trader: 05 mid.
Sales: Go to the market please.
Trader: You want me to buy the rest at the current level?
Sales: Yes please.
Trader: Sure… 20 done at 08. Your average is 06.4
Sales: OK to confirm, the client buys 25 EUR/USD at 1.25064
Trader: Agreed!

CHAPTER FOUR

THE GAME

This part is the most entertaining part of all, at least for me. A game played by not only the FX Traders, also by many different people in FX and Financial Markets. Once you understand how the game works, you will have a very good grasp of how the markets actually work. Then you can even apply it to your daily life, you can play it with your colleagues, friends and family. To understand the rules of the game, let's first go on with the Treasurer case. We will need to add some new words to our terminology before we start playing the game. Once again, I will skip the conversation between the Sales and the Treasurer and assume Sales is already talking on behalf of the treasurer.

Sales: I need a price in 40 Cable please.
(Client needs a price for 40 million GBP/USD)
Trader: Sure. 52/60
The following answers by Sales all have the same meaning which is client wants to BUY.
Sales: **Mine!**
 At 60 please!
 I pay you!
 I buy!
 On the right!
 Right-hand-side please!
 You lose them!

Similarly, if the client wanted to SELL, the following answers would suit the situation.

Sales: **Yours!**
      At 52 please!
      I give you!
      I sell!
      On the left!
      Left-hand-side please!
      You get them!

Once you get used to it, words will come out of your mouth with no effort, however, many new joiners find it confusing at the beginning. As an example, *"You lose them!"* is not something we normally think as if someone has bought something from us. Among the list above, "MINE and YOURS" are the ones which are used more often than the others.

Please think over the following conversation, and if you fully understand what is written immediately, I can say you already speak the language of the markets at the least to the level where you can play the Game.

Trading head walks over to the desk 20 minutes after hearing about the flow.

Head: *How did the cable flow go?*
Trader: It was alright, I was given at 52. Cable dumped initially but I didn't panic really. **It didn't feel heavy** *at all lately and particularly today it was bid all day long.*
Head: *Where did you get out then?*
Trader: I sticked an offer at 55 initially, lost the first half there and offered the balance at 57 where I was **lifted** *in one clip.*

The meaning of the language used above apart from the last few words should already be relatively obvious. "...*offered the balance at 57 where I was lifted in one clip."* means he tried to sell the remaining amount at 57, and one single counterparty bought (lifted) all of it in one go.

Now, instead of going through the details of the game, I will instead write a made-up scenario which should make the rules clear. There are unlimited number of versions to set as the underlying of the game, but a very common one is an unhealthy option where a person in the office volunteers to eat as many cookies (lollies, burgers, etc.) as possible in a given time frame. Usually this person would be among the juniors who wants to become famous, impress the seniors or someone who wants to have some fun. Please note there is usually little to none at stake for the bets. It is not about money but rather it is about being right, winning and fun.

Maria: OK! I'll take the challenge for the cookies.

James: Cookies are on me then.

Andy: Let's put a dollar per cookie.

George: How many do you think can you eat Maria in one hour?

Maria: 20?

George: Yours! (The game did not start here yet, it is just that George thinks Maria cannot eat as many as 20.)

Isabel: I know she is slim but, I have seen how much she can eat when she wants to.

George: She is not gonna eat salad, these are cookies.

Isabel: OK, make me a price then.

George: 11/18

Andy: Come on! That is too wide!

George: OK, I'll make you 12-14.

Isabel: Mine!

Andy: I pay you there as well if still valid.

George: Fine I lost at 14 to both of you. You will see, I won't even need to cover.

Isabel: I will call the strategy guy, he was there when we had that big dinner. (Speakerphone) - Hey Mike, we are doing a cookie challenge here, it is 1 dollar per cookie. How many do you think Maria can eat in one hour?

Mike: She can eat a lot! OK I'll make you a price.

Isabel: We started making 2 wide here.

Mike: Hmm. I don't know what the market is up there. But I will make you 22-24.

Isabel: Yours!
Mike: Did I make an **off-market price?**
Isabel: As a matter of fact, I would make a similar price but currently, yes, your price is off market.

So, what just happened there? Isabel bought "it" at 14 and sold it at 22. And what is "it" again? Maria didn't even start eating the cookies yet. James haven't even bought them! But Isabel locked in an 8 pips/cookies/dollar profit already. The game goes on for a few hours until Maria finds some empty space in her stomach later in the afternoon. Tens of people make bets on the price which stabilizes around 22 in the end and Maria finally starts eating. She ends up eating 15 cookies, leaving George's uncovered short position at 14 with one-dollar loss (two dollars in total as he agreed with two people at that price). As many people got involved, George was made fun of for hours because of his lower than average price and he was the first person to make that "ridiculous" price. He ended up with a dollar loss per contract, still better than many others who seemed to have better fun for the last few hours. On the other hand, Isabel thought Maria could do better than 15 and she locked in a profit because she was **bullish** (thinking that the market will go higher) at the time when the price was 12-14 expecting to price to go higher. In the following hours another guy who sold the high of the market, say, at 27 was **bearish** expecting the market to find a balance lower than 27 and either locked in a profit lower or waited till the end of the game making his profit of 12 dollars.

What is the lesson to be learned? Well, I will leave it up to you, as my sole purpose was to explain how this common game is played. As mentioned earlier, the underlying can take different forms as there are many different currency pairs in the market. If the cookie is the EUR/USD, chicken nuggets could be the GBP/USD where the correlation is expected to be high, whereas EUR/CZK could look like an underlying of this game where the bet is on how many people will have lunch after 1 p.m. (there is still a correlation but relatively less than the former case. I have seen this game played on the number of seats an opposition party will get in a parliament after an election. You can extend the list to the limit of your imagination.

CHAPTER FIVE

MARKET PARTICIPANTS

FX is a giant area in Financial Industry and there are many different types of market participants. If your aim is to be a professional in this industry, you might consider working for some of these market participants, I will be talking about some of the important market participants but it is literally impossible to cover all of them as one might argue that every single person and institution in the planet somehow can be considered as a direct or indirect market participant. This will not only be a list of participants, but, in between the lines, I will also be talking through some other topics which are essential for any market participant.

1) Central Banks: This will not be a list in any sort of order in terms of importance, but I wanted to mention Central Banks at the beginning because Central Banks are at the heart of Foreign Exchange Markets and I will be writing about them in more detail than the others. What is more interesting is that their impact usually comes in an indirect manner as opposed to direct market involvement. Unless preannounced, you won't see a Central Bank buying or selling Foreign Exchange in the market every day. And if you see, there is a good chance of that hitting the news/headlines. Technically, Central Banks are very powerful institutions in terms of their trading volume 'potential' if they choose to make a direct involvement. If you go to a random Central Bank's website, it is very likely that you will find how much **reserves** they have. You will notice that these reserves are mostly USDs, Gold and Euros. These are followed by other precious metals and other currencies.

If a Central Bank wants to appreciate the value of its own currency, it can use its reserves to sell into the market. However, this comes with a risk which is depletion of its reserves. It is very common for Central Banks, especially the EM ones, to keep their reserves for emergency situations although this does not have to be the case. If there is no reserve and the interest in the country's currency is going down, this might cause a crisis. The reserves are to be kept for those days.

On the other hand, if a Central Bank wants to depreciate the value of its own currency, it can technically buy as many foreign currencies as it wants because Central Banks are the authorities to print their own currencies to the limit of their own decision as an independent organization. Here, a very common question asked is why a Central Bank would do that to its own currency. First, we need to understand that when buying foreign currencies, depreciation might not be the actual target of the Central Bank. Maybe the Central Bank only wanted to increase its reserves for the bad times. And second, we need to understand that a weaker currency does not necessarily mean a bad thing and likewise a strong currency does not necessarily mean a good thing. Furthermore, a stronger currency might be good for someone and a bad for another both living in the same country. Importers vs exporters is an excellent example to remember if there is any confusion. Let's imagine exporter's situation in a stronger currency situation. An exporter is selling a product to US for five dollars. His own currency is ABC and it costs 8 ABC to produce the product. USD/ABC rate is 2.00. Five dollars will mean 10 ABCs, so the exporter's net profit is 2 ABCs. Another exporter in a different country sells the same product to US for five dollars as well with the XYZ currency. Imagine that ABC strengthens against USD and 1 USD is 1.6ABC and not 2 ABC anymore. It will cost 8 ABC to produce and 5 dollars will bring the exporter 8 ABC back. There is no profit anymore.

ABC either needs to stop exporting or increase the price to, say six dollars. But there is the other challenge here. Exporter in XYZ already sells the same product for five dollars, why would US buy it from ABC anymore?

I hope this is clear, so going back to Central Banks' activities in terms of weakening a country's own currency, good recent examples have been in Switzerland and Czech Republic, where both Central Banks set a **floor** for their currencies using the EUR as a base as they kept buying Euros in the market when the market reached to their floor level so that their own currency could not appreciate more. Having talked about one risk of selling reserves, I might need to mention at least one risk to buying reserves but I will leave it up to you to search for Swiss Floor and you might see interesting stories online. Risk to whom is a different question though.

So, if the direct involvement is not the most frequent way the Central Banks operate, then what is it? Central Banks come with important decisions and publish important documents like inflation reports. A central bank is normally expected to be an independent organization as mentioned. No matter what view the government has, the Central Banks are expected to make their own decisions. If you have studied economics you would already have a broad understanding of the interest rates and I won't be going through the importance of the interest rate decision on economy here. If you have no idea about it, for now, bear in mind that for any market participant, the interest rate meetings of Central Banks are usually the most important things to watch for any given country's currency.

The immediate impact on the currency of these decisions are at a minimum of 3 stages. All 3 have to be considered together though. To exemplify, let's say country ABC has interest rate of 3%.
   1. A **hike** (let's say to 3.25%) is likely to make the ABC currency appreciate, whereas <u>a **cut**</u> (let's say to 2.75%) is likely to make the ABC currency depreciate. (Given everything else is similar and unchanged in two

different economies, you are expected to bring your cash to the country which offers a higher interest rate)

2. Market expectations vs the actual decision: This is important for all sorts of data and particularly for the interest rate decisions. If a hike to 3.75% is expected in the above example and only 3.25% is done, you won't be that likely to see ABC appreciating and furthermore there would be a good chance of depreciation.

3. Central Bank Statements: Let's assume market expectation was for a hike of 25 **Basis Points** (which is from 3.00% to 3.25%) and the Central Bank hikes 50 Basis Points (which is from 3.00% to 3.50%). Based on what you have read earlier, you would normally expect to see the confluence of the two points earlier and expect currency to appreciate, right? What if the market expectation was for a **hike cycle** of 25 basis points for the next 5 meetings eventually reaching to 4.25% but instead the Central Bank hiked 50 basis points and, in their statement, they said they won't be hiking again for the next few years. Wouldn't it be a totally different story?

2) Banks: The relevant departments within Banks are the places where the big volumes of currencies are exchanged. Depending on the internal structure of any bank, you might see the largest volumes in divisions like Treasury, Markets and Investment Bank units. Due to different reasons such as legal ones and access to better platforms, banks usually provide an easier execution option for other market participants. If a fund wants to sell a few hundred million of a currency pair, you will see them calling a salesperson in a bank as the trader in the bank will have access to different platforms which he/she can find better liquidity.

3) Buy Side: This is generally the client group of the Banks. Hedge Funds, Pension Funds, Asset Managements are some of the Buy Side group of Financial Markets. The research done in these institutions are done for the institutions' own benefit where only group members utilize as opposed to publicly available research provided by different companies such as Banks. As an example, the PMs or traders or any other decision maker in a Hedge Fund will decide on what currency pair to buy or sell and will usually call a bank to execute the transaction in the market. The purpose of this transaction comes from a view that the decision maker has. Say, the fund manager buys EUR/USD. This might be due to the fact that he/she thinks the EUR/USD is going higher, it might also be due to the fact that he is already short, say, GBP/USD and he/she wants to partially hedge the USD risk by going long in EUR/USD. Eventually the fund's sole purpose is to make money for the clients with the fund's own views of the markets.

4) Corporates: In this group, especially the multinationals are the crucial contributors to the market in terms of providing the market with both colour and liquidity. This is where one of the biggest real interest come from instead of the interest from speculators in the industry. A multinational corporate, say in US, will eventually have to convert some of the cash earned in other countries to USDs for accounting purposes. On the other hand, it might be investing in a foreign country where it needs to convert the USDs to the local currency. These are only two simple way of looking at things they do although Treasury Departments could be working on these transactions for more complicated hedging purposes.

5) Brokers: Brokers match the interests of Banks (but not necessarily limited to Banks) in different forms. Say Bank A wants to sell a financial instrument. It is usually better and easier for him to go to a broker whose job is to find a buyer than call banks one by one to see if there is anyone who would be interested in buying. The activity of the brokers can be over the telephone, chat rooms or simply online matching systems where there is little to no human involvement. The broker takes a commission for matching the two counterparties. Some people think it is similar to being a real estate agent. Although, there are similarities in terms of the pay structure, different skill sets are required for these two professions. I find it similar to saying a trader's job in a bank is similar to someone working in a grocery shop. Yes, there are similarities, but these require different skill sets.

There are three questions that I am very often asked. First one usually comes from the layman which is: "What is the difference between a trader and a broker?". The answer to this should be very obvious by now and the second question is: "What is the difference between **Hedge Funds** and **Prop Trading Houses**?" Before answering that let me tell you one last question which usually comes from people who are already educated or experienced in the markets: "What is the difference between traders working for different organizations?" First, we need to define the job of an FX Trader. An FX Trader can work for a Bank, A Hedge Fund or a Prop Trading House among others including working for himself/herself. A Trader tries to make money in mainly two ways. First one is from the flows as mentioned earlier. And second one is through prop trading where the trader bets on the market, trying to buy low, sell high. A trader in a Hedge Fund (although you will commonly see PMs and execution traders separately, all I am referring to is the decision maker by using the broad term trader) and a trader in a Prop Trading House both try to make money on their market views, they will not have flows like the Bank Traders do, so prop trading is their only option. A trader in a Hedge Fund uses various clients'/investors' funds to go into these transactions, whereas prop trading houses usually consist of smaller groups which employ traders to manage their own funds. Depending on the country a hedge fund is located, there could be limits to minimum funds a client needs to invest for a hedge fund to accept managing the funds, so you will often hear the total funds under control reaches billions in many hedge funds whereas Prop Trading Houses are more limited in terms of funds under management. For a trader, since the volumes and risk and thus the potential earnings are seen as limited in Prop Trading Houses, you shouldn't be surprised to see Prop Trading Houses offering significant cuts of the money made by traders to attract good ones to their companies. Unlike many other organizations, including the banks, sales force is not at the heart of the organization either in a Prop Trading House. Also marketing costs would be limited if there is any, so it is not unwise to allocate resources to talented traders.

We need to be clear that, unlike the layman's guess on the industry, trading is not the only way to make a living in this industry, and it is not necessarily the highest paying job. There are several different functions, departments inside any of these market participant institutions. Being a broker, working in operations, working in sales force, being a research analyst, a strategist are only a few options to consider out of many.

There are reasons to why this conception of trading and Forex Markets go hand in hand as if the rest do not get involved in important business decisions. Traders being on newspapers in both the best and the worst times is one reason to that and also easiness of access to individual trading is a significant factor that added to this conception. I have not listed individual traders as major market participants; however, it is true that there hasn't been an easier time to work as an individual trader. This easiness is only about access to markets though, making a life on FX trading is not easy at all. When you search online, go to social media and search for FX, you will see many trainers who try to teach people how to trade the Forex Markets. I am not saying they do it on purpose, but they clearly contribute to this misconception as well as to the misconception of trading being easy. The good thing is they have to put disclaimers before their trainings start. As an experienced trader, I urge you to read the disclaimers carefully as I believe they will give you a more important message than the training itself.

Although individual trading is very different than all the other options to make a living through FX as stated above, and although there are many statistics (I have no idea about how accurate they are) showing that over 90% of the individual traders losing money, people still want to trade and many people are using online services to access the Forex Markets. I also believe that without training, making a living on trading FX is close to impossible, however, I am here neither to suggest any trading instructor nor to give a trading training to you on my own. On the other hand, I also believe at a minimum level these trainings should be provided by experienced traders. That is one of the reasons you should read those disclaimers again and again as the person you are getting your training from might not have any experience at all. If you already have read the book up to here, you should have already noticed that many of those people don't even use or know about the market language. I am not suggesting that "If you speak the market language, you are assured to make a living" or "If you can't speak the language, you won't be able to generate any profits", but all I am saying is my personal preferences on two things when I get a training on any topic. 1) I prefer to get it from someone who has the experience on the topic he/she is teaching. 2) I prefer to be trained by someone who has a full grasp of what he is talking about.

There is no difference to FX and any other topic. If you are reading a self-help book, or a finance book, say on how to build a thriving business, I suggest you pick the author with a considerable track record of building businesses.

CHAPTER SIX

ARE THE ADVANTAGES OF FX MARKETS REAL?

Among other things in disclaimers, *"... Losses can exceed the initial deposit…"* is particularly important and I don't think it is fully regarded. Especially in the short term, it seems less likely to have an awful experience in FX trading due to the so-called advantages of trading FX vs other products. I said "it seems", but let's see together how much these advantages really matter, and ask this question to ourselves: Are the advantages real?

One of the advantages frequently mentioned comes with the liquidity. It is true that the volumes in FX Markets are more than any other thing in Financial Markets. Total daily volume in FX Markets is said to be between 3 to 5 trillion dollars. This large volume gives the markets a relatively good liquidity compared to other markets on a normal day. If we are to make a comparison with the stock market, you are likely to buy a currency pair at the first price you see without making an impact in the market unless you are a very big player, but a similar size clip might change the prices in stock markets quicker in the short term. I am not arguing against this advantage, yet. Please read on.

Second advantage mentioned is that it is easy to find an online service which gives people the availability to **leverage** their position sizes. You must already be familiar with the term and in FX Markets, if a service provider offers you a 100 leverage, that means if you were to take, say 1 million USD/JPY position, you only have to deposit 10,000 dollars. If the leverage is 200, you can take positions up to 200 times of your deposit and so on... This clearly makes the FX world look very attractive but the truth is the larger your leverage is the larger your risks are. If you leverage yourself 100 times, just over a 1% move in the currency pair is enough to clear your balance and 1% move is not even an extreme move in currency markets.

Third thing that seems like an advantage is that FX Markets are open 24 hours excluding weekends. This means you are more likely to get protected if there is a sudden move in the market. Say a stock is trading 200ABC per share in the country of ABC. With some bad news overnight, you might see the share price opening at 190, 180 maybe 170, or simply **limit down.** Limit down, is the minimum price a stock can trade down to in a single day before trading restrictions trigger. FX Markets, being open 24 hours a day is more likely to give you an option to prevent losses. Yes, there is a theoretical advantage but it doesn't guarantee anything at all. Moreover, this logic sometimes gives a wrong impression that traders can take a stop loss whenever they wanted to which leads people to take larger risks than think they do. When a new home-based trader reads the *"... Losses can exceed the initial deposit..."* line he/she might wrongly think, "Oh, if I deposit USD 500 I might lose 550 USD, I can afford USD 50 more, let's give it a try". Search for "Swiss Floor" or "GBP flash crash" and you will see two different real-life examples where the liquidity went to extremely low levels. OK, imagine two different scenarios around the time EURCHF floor had been removed. (If you have not searched for it online, to give you a basic idea of the price action, it didn't take too long for EURCHF to trade below 1.0000 levels all the way from 1.2000). Scenario 1: You are long EURCHF, you have 1.1950 Stop Loss order with your broker. You think you are risking 500 euros with that position. After the floor is removed, the first price that your broker can sell your position is 1.10.

Result: Your loss is many multiple times you thought it would be. Scenario 2: You are long EURCHF, you have 1.1950 Stop Loss order with your broker. Broker guarantees a 10 pip stop loss which is in worst case, the broker assures you to sell your position out at 1.1940 if there is a big market move. Floor is removed. The first price your broker can get you out is 1.05. But the broker assured you to give you a **fill** at 1.1940. No surprises, the broker assured a few hundred more people. I won't go on with the rest, if you were in that situation, you might have needed a lawyer much more than a financial adviser.

CHAPTER SEVEN

TRADERS' TOOLS

So, how do the traders make money then? Once again, I am not here to suggest any form of training on how to make money through trading, but I will be writing about some of the tools traders utilize. To be consistent with this book's structure, I will continue to elaborate on terminology without going too deep into detail when we come across to something I have not mentioned before. If you decide on learning the topics stated below in more detail and if you want to understand what the potential ways to take advantage of those, please remember to read disclaimers first.

A trader's main objective is to generate **PnL** with the minimum risk assigned to it, or at least within the risk limits. **PnL** or **P&L** is simply the **Profit and Loss** statement. It is the scorecard of a trader. PnLs in institutions are mostly checked on a daily, monthly, quarterly and yearly basis. Companies that pay out bonuses to employees based on the PnL mostly look at the yearly PnLs and traders working for those companies will be checking their YTD (Year-to-date) PnL every single day. Even some big companies made the mistake of judging the traders based purely on the PnL in the past, without looking at the risk taken, PnL on its own does not mean too much. A trader in a hedge fund might generate 1 million dollars a year managing 10 million dollars and another might generate 5 million dollars a year managing 100. Does it make the 5 million PnL trader more successful than the other? Certainly not. You might say who cares if the bonuses are paid based purely on the PnL. Yes, many companies made that mistake ending up finding traders gambling by taking too big risks to make money one year only to end up with losses another year. Nowadays, risk based PnL measures such as Sharpe Ratios - which are too much of a detail to be elaborated in this book - are taken into account more often.

Risk calculations are not only at the company level, traders are also individually monitored. Traders also monitor their own risks with different measures. One common measure used in FX Trading is the **Risk/Reward Ratio**. This ratio simply compares how much a trader is willing to make and how much of a loss the he/she is willing to accept if the trade goes against the trader. This calculation can be made both in monetary terms and pip terms. If you are long EUR/USD which you bought at 1.2000, you decide to take a stop at 1.1900 (if you can) and your target is at 1.2200, your Risk/Rewards Ratio is simply 1:2. It is marketed that if you have such a Risk/Reward Ratio or better and if you are right half of the time, your earnings potential is significant. It is not something that doesn't makes sense, on the other hand, it is not hundred percent true either. First of all, please remember any stop loss orders are subject to "if you can" as I earlier wrote in brackets and I don't think it is emphasized enough by trading instructors and coaches but rather it is assumed that you always have this availability. Secondly, let's assume that you really can, by experience and talking to different people who has experience, I can tell you that taking a stop is not the easiest thing in the world. It requires an extremely disciplined mind, even for very experienced traders. There are reasons to it, where hope is the most common one. On top of that experienced traders have many times came across to situations where their stops are triggered and market turned after that very point. These kinds of experiences might lead to traders being more stubborn on their positions (**married to their positions** in markets language). Again, by experience, only people I saw who have made money on a consistent basis are the ones who have sticked to their rules. Thirdly, there is something which I call **The Stop Loss Illusion.** I wrote this in bold, but it is not a term used in the market, the only reason I made it bold is because I think you should be aware of this when you are watching or listening to a training. You will see some people will say "My Risk/Reward Ratio is 1:1, but there is a very big probability that I am right." I have nothing to say against the belief in probabilities but a Risk/Reward ratio is usually tweaked to one side, because it is very likely that you will find yourself filled at the exact target level, if things go in your favour, if not, there is a good chance that you won't be filled at the exact stop level. There is a stop loss illusion that as if it was guaranteed (unless it is really guaranteed, but that not only comes with another risk for large price movements as mentioned earlier, but also it usually comes with a fee to guarantee your level). For closer target and stop levels, this matters even more and the impact is amplified even more with the less liquid currency pairs. In any case, a 1:1 Risk Reward is never an exact 1:1. So you will require much higher probabilities of being right than 50%.

When the matter is generating trade ideas, traders use two main tools. **Fundamentals** and **Technicals. Fundamentals** answer the question "How good is..." A country's currency will tell you a lot about that country's economy, fiscal and monetary policies, political situation and even the level of democracy and life quality. That is the main reason why the risk element for EM currencies is much higher and thus the liquidity is lower and the spreads are wider. These are all under the topic of fundamentals. If you search for economic calendars, you will see a bunch of data lined up for different countries and anything you see there will go under fundamentals. Inflation prints, growth numbers, unemployment figures, interest rate decisions, industrial outputs, PMI numbers are just to name a few of them. If you go to a random professional in the Forex world and ask "What is the single most important data print in the world?" There is a good chance that he/she replies back with **US Non-Farm Payroll (NFP).** This is a measure for number of paid workers excluding a group of employees, farm workers being one as the name suggests. The number is usually released on the first Friday of each month. There is a silence on trading floors of banks and possibly some other institutions right before the number is released. When the number is out, the currency markets experience one of the most volatile short-term price actions. Just like any other data, expectations vs. the actual number is crucial for market participants.

Technicals, on the other hand are purely about the price action in the market. Charts are used to determine the trading views here. There is a myriad of possible terminology to be used looking at only one simple chart and I will only mention a few here. I am sure you have heard the terms **support** and **resistance.** A **support**, is where - just looking at a chart - there seems to be an interest to buy a currency pair (or any other market). A **resistance**, is where - just looking at a chart - there seems to be an interest to sell a currency pair (or any other market). Support and resistance might be trending instead of sitting on one single level. This is where you will hear the terms **trendline support** and **trendline resistance**.

Whenever you hear these terms or **candlestick bars** (a charting method), **Fibonacci Retracement Levels** (a method of determining levels in the market), **patterns, breakouts**,..you are hearing about technicals. There is no single correct way to use the levels though, and some people will say, *"if we touch this support, it is a signal to buy"* or *"this is one of the patterns the price will go higher"* or *"if we break above this trendline resistance, market will go higher"*. None of these are 100% accurate, it is only that some people will assert they are right more often than they are wrong.

You will see traders being more (and sometimes only) interested in fundamentals and some others in technicals. Funny enough, some of the former group does not believe in technicals and vice versa. A very good friend of mine who has a Masters Degree in Finance once said to me "If I was to believe in technicals, I would have to tear my Masters Diploma off"

The following is my very personal opinion.

<< A trader can be inclined towards one of them, but no one can do without the other. It matters whether you believe in a level or you don't believe only because you think technicals make no sense. But what matters more is how many people believe in that level. You will see a price touching a level and bounce back several times in random time differences. A non-believer in technicals could hardly explain that kind of a price action. Of course, if you include supply and demand inside the fundamental analysis, you can still say something about it, but *why at that particular level* is the question to be asked.

On the other hand, some traders say that they never use fundamentals because they make no sense. First of all, you can observe that over the long term, many things make sense using fundamentals. And secondly, ask those traders whether they keep similar positions right before the data points. The answer will be NO. They will say, but they only trade on technicals. Experienced traders say "Sometimes, not trading is the best trading decision". If you are deciding on not trading, or reducing your sizes, amending your target and S/L levels based on an upcoming data, you are including fundamentals in your trading.>>

There is one last point I cannot do without mentioning. It is an illusion which is commonly mistaken by even the experienced professionals and moreover even by the experienced traders who should always be on top everything they are doing. The illusion comes with the calculation of a "potential PnL" from a trade. Please refer to Chapter 2 for the detailed calculation if you need. But at least it would be good to read the following very carefully, especially if you are reading this book to prepare for an interview. You know that it is very common for an interview to include a tricky question. If I was the interviewer, especially for a junior trading position, instead of asking tricky questions like those asked in consulting interviews, I would ask a simple PnL calculation. Question is this: "If you bought 1 million of USD/ZAR (if you bought one dollar rand) and USD/ZAR went 10% higher, how much money did you make?" The answer seems very obvious, as 10% of 1 million is 100,000. But it is wrong, and again unfortunately even the experienced people very often fall into this trap. To understand this better, think of the extreme cases. What if it was 100% higher, and what if 1000% higher? The answer is simple, you cannot make more than 1 million USD on a 1 million USD <u>long</u> position, no matter what. If you are working for a South African company which reports its PnL in ZAR, then percentage calculation might be a different case, but otherwise, if you are to give a quick answer and if you were to calculate your PnL in USDs or something relatively stable against USD, then the percentage increase is only an indicator to your actual PnL. Say, spot USD/ZAR rate was 10 and it moved to 12.5. This is 25% increase but your profit is actually 2.5 million ZAR amount. With the new rate it is worth 200,000 USDs (2,500,000/12.5=200,000). Your PnL is up 20%. Say, it moved from 10 to 20, a 100% increase will give you 10 million ZAR PnL which is 500,000 in USD terms with the new exchange rate (10,000,000/20=500,000). 100% increase in the exchange rate gives you 50% in PnL. So the smaller the percentage increase is, the closer your PnL to percentage moves, but never equal. This is valid for any currency that you base your calculations on and where you are long that currency on a winning position. In the USD/ZAR example above, when USD/ZAR rate goes lower, as you are long the ZAR, your ZAR based PnL cannot be more than the initial ZAR amount. Bottomline is that you can never be long one currency and make more PnL than that position size in that currency terms.

CHAPTER EIGHT

FX PRODUCTS AND DEPARTMENTS

Spot FX, is the most commonly known FX product in the world. However, FX Markets are way bigger than the spot market alone. **FX Forwards/Swaps** and **FX Options** are two of them among the important ones. In relatively small institutions, these products can all be traded by a single desk, however in large institutions there are different desks assigned to trading these different products. It would be good to mention that there are similar differences in sales desks as well. Depending on the organization, a sales desk can be structured based on the product they are selling. It can also be structured based on the client group that are being served. In the latter case, sales people can be involved in trading of various products but serving one particular client group. If you are working as a salesperson for a large bank, it would be very common for you to be in either Bank Sales where client group is purely banks, FI Sales (Financial Institutions) which might include the Bank Sales function but also covers for the buy side type of clients (Hedge Funds, Real Money), Corporate Sales where the client group is corporates (usually multinational corporates) which have real interest in currency markets rather than being speculative market participants. Among these, FI Sales is the one which is mostly confused. You will see people applying for Fixed Income Sales positions (which is of course possible), but only to find out that FI Sales position was meant for Financial Institutions Sales.

Going back to product types, it will be good to mention the **value date** here, which is simply the date where the exchange of the currencies are done. Unlike an exchange office on the street, exchange of FX Spot transactions mostly happen 2 days after the trade is done, (this is called **Value T+2)**. You will also find some currencies like CAD, RUB and TRY having spot dates 1 day after the trade is done (**Value T+1).** There might be confusion of the value dates when we talk about **crosses,** and it is always good to check value dates on those. As an example, not being a rule, market generally trades spot EUR/RUB as T+1, whereas spot EUR/TRY is traded T+2 more often. When there is a trade of **baskets,** it might be even more confusing. A currency basket is where the value of a currency is determined by measuring against more than one currency with either equal or different weightings. RUB and TRY baskets, are both famous ones and it is always good to check for the value date details, whether you are trading it or somehow related to the trade. Accuracy and timeliness of these transactions are crucial for the stability of financial markets. This is where the Back-Office functions of Financial Institutions carry big importance.

FX Forwards/Swaps Desks, are mostly interested in value dates other than the spot. In academic studies, there is a distinction between an FX Swap and an FX Forward. The difference is that, in the former one, you exchange a currency pair in one day and at an agreed rate you exchange them back. As an example, 1-month EUR/USD swap could be like this: You buy EUR/USD at the spot date and sell it back 1 month after the spot date at an agreed price. Here, the interest differential is more important than the spot exchange rate movements. Unless there is a big movement in the spot rate, it only matters to determine the swap points based on the interest rate. (I won't go through the calculations here but you can find them online or in a very basic finance book easily.) On the other hand, an FX Forward, according to academic studies, determines the rate at which you can buy or sell a currency pair today with a value date in the future. In the real FX world however, Forward and Swap are two terms used interchangeably. To reflect the "FX Forward" concept as used in academics, in FX Markets, **"FX Forward Outright"** is the term used instead.

One last point to make is that, not all of the currencies are deliverable, which means, exchange of every currency pair in the world is not possible. However, some of them are still available to market participants and market for these are significantly large. These are what we call the **NDFs** which stand for **Non-Deliverable Forwards.** I don't want to bore you with details by elaborating on detail where I need to explain terms like fixing and how these are calculated, but as a basic rule you should know that these are traded on a forward (outright) basis where the difference in the agreed price to the real price on the value date is paid from one counterparty to the other with a deliverable currency such as USDs and EURs.

A FINAL NOTE

Once again, I strongly believe, if you are to take part in this giant industry, you MUST know what you have read so far. As you have noticed, I wrote the terminology used in the FX Markets in bold. You might want to revisit those in bold especially if you are new to the industry or you are preparing for an interview in the industry. Otherwise, if you require more information on the topics, the ones in bold could be a good guidance for you to know what exactly to search for.

This book was not only about the terminology used in the markets, but I also have provided you with the insights on how the markets actually work. I encourage you to revisit Chapter 4 – THE GAME, to be comfortable on understanding what is happening in the trading world.

I hope you enjoyed this book, and if you require more information, please do not hesitate to contact me on umutsasoglu@umbaba.net

Printed in Great Britain
by Amazon